TASTE

A TASTE OF DREAM WITH HIGHLIGHTS AND RECIPES

S. Q. ORPIN

Published by Wild Hibiscus Press

PO Box 1761 Lafayette CA 94549

Cover created by Fresh Design

TASTE is dedicated to my culinary friends who continually inspire me and always turn an event into a party.

THE CATWALK SERIES

The Catwalk series was inspired by the exciting but perilous world of modeling in Los Angeles. Dream was motivated by an accident that redefined the life of the author's model-niece, Sterling. Wanting to give a voice to additional characters and in response to a 'What next?' storyline, Catwalk expanded to a five-part series. The stories encompass a deep examination of characters struggling to find meaning in life and love. The books explore the diverse characters, while delving into the deep, and sometimes dark, human existence and tumultuous relationships. The series contains adult situations and language, including sex, trauma, and violence.

Dream introduces the cast of characters and the relationship developing between Casi and Kyle. It layers the superficial world of modeling with the lifestyle of a small-town man, creating challenges and pitfalls. **Hope** continues as reality and conflict consume the couple and supporting character storylines develop. **Trust** explores the emotional rollercoaster of love, career, loss, and coming to terms with the past. **Seek** reveals secrets and back story, helping the characters move forward as emotional scars are healed. **Love** is the final book in the series which spans five years, achieving triumph and a sense of belonging. The series primarily focuses on the main characters of Casi and Kyle, but additional characters are intricately woven throughout the five books.

Throughout the series, cooking is an integral part of the story. From Kyle, who is a passionate cook and dated a chef, to Casi who lacks interest in the entire process. Cooking and enjoying a meal together is a way for the characters to express themselves and enrich their lives.

DREAM- BOOK ONE IN THE CATWALK SERIES

Opposite worlds collide after a tragic accident and a chance encounter. Is it a twist of fate or a fatal mistake?

In a world of glitz and excess, sizzling-hot Casi Roberts is the reigning queen. Swimsuit model by day and club girl by night, she floats through Los Angeles on the arm of her celebrity artist boyfriend, Alix Grey, documenting her fabulous life on social media.

The illusion of perfection is shattered after an accident leaves her with physical scars, while emotional scars surface from her troubled past.

Casi's tenuous relationship with her drug-addled mother, Sonya, continues to undermine her confidence as she struggles to find balance in a chaotic business obsessed with youth and beauty.

Ruggedly handsome, master craftsman, Kyle Jensen is cool, calm, and collected. He has built an enviable life in Blackberry Falls, WA, while keeping his troubled older brother, Jake, in line. After a passionate encounter with Casi, Kyle's carefully crafted life begins to unravel, making him question the plan he had for his future.

Can Casi step away from the spotlight and take a chance on love and explore new opportunities?

Will Kyle risk his idyllic life to follow his heart?

Do they dare to dream of a future together?
Dream available on Amazon

Dare to Dream, Hope, Trust, Seek, and most of all, Love.

CAST OF CHARACTERS

Casi Roberts: A swimsuit model in LA. Born in Burnaby, Canada.

Kyle Jensen: A master woodworker with his own business in Washington State.

Jake: Kyle's older brother and business partner.

Gail: Jake's wife and mother of his two children.

Reid: Jake's son.

Olivia: Jake's daughter.

Jack Roberts: Casi's father. He owns a restaurant and brewery in Bellingham, WA. Divorced from Casi's mother, Sonya. Married to Ava.

Ava: Jack's wife and Casi's stepmother.

Mary: Casi's mentor and Ava's close friend.

Sonya: Casi's troubled mother.

Georgia Jensen: Kyle's and Jake's adoptive mother.

Peter Jensen: Married to Georgia, and the adoptive father of Kyle and Jake.

Tara: Biological mother of Kyle and Jake.

Earl: Peter's best friend and former partner in a plumbing business.

Libby: Peter's sister. She is a writer and lives all over the world.

Alix: Casi's ex-boyfriend. Celebrity graphic artist.

Dylan: Casi's best friend in LA. Also her hairdresser.

Ray Dawson: Casi's doorman in LA. He is an avid cook.

Nadia: Model, artist, and supplier of pain pills.

Alejandro: Soccer player who dated Casi.

Johan: Owner of the Sand and Surf line.

Joey: Casi's high school boyfriend.

Dawn: Casi's best friend from childhood

Lia: Lauren's older sister.

Lauren: Lia's sister. Dated Kyle for three years. A chef in Seattle.

Fran: The mother of Lia and Lauren.

Mary Ann: Gail's best friend.

Robert: Works in Bellingham at the Brewery. Riley's brother.

Riley: The apprentice at the wood shop.

Amy: The receptionist at the wood shop. Dating Riley.

Anna: A lumber rep in Seattle. Briefly dated Kyle.

Grady: Kyle's best friend from high school who was killed in a boating accident.

Brian: The Jensen brother's accountant.

Jezebel: Casi's calico cat.

Dingo: Kyle's German short-haired dog.

1

BACKSTAGE

"Three minutes, girls!" belted the overbearing Mary Anderson, more lovingly referred to as Mother Mary, by the models of Beyond Modeling Agency. With the efficiency of a drill sergeant and the tenderness of a mother, Mary consistently produced a bobby pin or tissue, ready to wipe a tear or redirect a negative attitude.

Casi smoothed her hand over her sleek, waist-length, espresso brown hair as the artist reapplied stage makeup. The heavy black eyeliner, creating the quintessential 'smoky eye,' overpowered her hazel eyes and gentle features. Encased in a black and gray leather dress with too many zippers, and six-inch, open-toed boots, she followed Mary's prompt toward the catwalk. As Casi confidently strutted on the stage, the model ahead started to wobble around a turn. Trying to recover from the misstep, the girl leaned right, balancing on one heel. The bored audience found a renewed interest in the impending disaster, cameras at the ready. Suddenly on her knees, breasts launched from their tape, and one ill-fitted stiletto dangling from her foot, the red-faced figure staggered to regain her composure. Casi sidestepped the train wreck with practiced ease, familiar with fallen deities.

MARY'S AUSTRIAN KRINGLE

Serves 8

Dough:

1 package (.25 ounce) active dry yeast

1/4 cup warm water

1/2 cup butter, cold and cut into ½-inch cubes

2 ¼ cups all-purpose flour

1/2 teaspoon salt

1 tablespoon sugar

1/2 cup milk, warmed to 110-degrees

1 egg, beaten

Filling:

1 1/2 cups almonds, finely chopped

1 cup dark brown sugar

1/2 cup butter, soft

Glaze:

1 cup powdered sugar

2 tablespoons heavy cream

1/2 teaspoon almond extract

¼ cup sliced almonds, toasted

1. In a small bowl, dissolve yeast in warm water. Let stand until foamy.

2. Combine flour, salt, and sugar in a large bowl and drop in the cubes of butter. Use a pastry blender or fork, to cut the butter into flour until particles are the size of small peas.

3. Add yeast mixture, warm milk, and egg; beat until smooth (dough will be soft). Cover and refrigerate for 2 hours.

4. In a medium bowl, mix the chopped almonds, brown sugar, and soft butter together. Set aside.

5. Remove the dough from the fridge. On a well-floured board, roll into a 15 x 10-inch rectangle, approximately 1/2-inch thick.

6. Spread the prepared nut filling down the center of the rolled-out dough, leaving a 3-inch border on either side. Fold sides of dough over filling, overlapping ½-inch. Pinch edges to seal.

7. Form roll into a circle and pinch ends together. Place seam side down on a sheet pan with parchment paper. Cover and let rise in a warm place for 30 minutes or until double in size.

8. Preheat oven to 350-degrees.

9. After the dough has risen, bake the Kringle for 20 minutes until golden brown or when the internal temperature registers approximately 200-degrees. Remove from oven and let cool for 15 minutes.

10. Mix the powdered sugar, cream, and almond extract until smooth. Add more cream if needed. Drizzle prepared glaze over the Kringle. Sprinkle with sliced almonds.

2

THE KISS

*C*asi walked past the apartment being remodeled, and the twang of country music caught her attention. The upbeat rhythm mixed with the heady scent of fresh-cut wood, and the desire to be part of the moment overcame her. She opened the door and strode confidently to the lean, muscular man, measuring a piece of wood on his makeshift workbench. He glanced up and gave her a half-smile, almost as if he had been expecting her. A smile touched her lips as she came within inches of him. Without thinking, she placed her hand to his strong jaw and brought his lips to meet her own. Bewilderment crossed his face, but he let her take the lead. His lips were firm and inviting, and the sensation awakened every cell in her body. She switched her brain off and pressed her chest against his, commanding the moment. He wrapped his arms around her, and she felt breathless and tingly. She caressed the smoothness of his skin, wanting so much more.

Coming to her senses, she jumped away and covered her face with her hands and he scanned her quizzically. Since first seeing him, she often fantasized about kissing him, imagining how he would taste and the warmth of his mouth on hers. Having acted on the impulse was another matter entirely.

CASI'S MONKEY BREAD

Serves 12

Dough:

2 1/2 teaspoons active dry yeast

1 cup warm water, 110-degrees

1/4 cup sugar

3 cups all-purpose flour

1 teaspoon ground cinnamon

1 teaspoon salt

2 tablespoons butter, melted

Sugar Mixture:

1 cup butter

1 cup packed brown sugar

1. Mix the yeast with the warm water and sugar and let sit for a few minutes until the mixture is foamy. Add the flour, cinnamon, salt, and 2 tablespoons melted butter and mix until the dough forms a soft ball, adding more flour if needed. Knead until smooth.
2. In a medium saucepan on low heat, melt one cup of butter, stir in brown sugar. Remove from heat.
3. Divide the dough into one-inch balls. Drop one piece at a time into the butter-brown sugar mixture, then layer loosely in a greased Bundt pan. Cover and let rise in a warm, draft-free spot until dough reaches the top of the pan, about 1 hour.
4. Bake in a preheated 350-degree oven for 20 to 25 minutes or till golden brown. Remove from oven and let cool for 5 minutes. Place a plate face down on top of the pan and, using oven mitts to hold plate on pan, turn over and transfer the bread to the plate.

3

DESIRE

"Peace offering," Casi said, putting the wine bottle on the bar with a radiant smile.

Kyle narrowed his eyes. "I'm unclear what game you're playing, but I'm not interested in your scam."

Ouch, that was well deserved. "I'm not sure what came over me the other day, and I apologize for what happened afterward. If you got to know me, you'd see I'm a much better person than that." She extended her hand confidently. "I'm Casi Roberts. I'm twenty-nine and a model since I was seventeen. I live in one of the third-floor apartments with my boyfriend, Alix Grey, a well-known artist. I should be at his reception, but I wanted to introduce myself properly."

A smile reached his eyes as he scanned her face. "Hello, Casi Roberts. I'm Kyle Jensen, from Blackberry Falls, Washington. I'm thirty-three, and obviously, a custom woodworker. Do you come here often?" He gave a slight chuckle at his pickup line.

"Only when I need to apologize for my bad behavior. So pretty much every Tuesday," she joked back, shaking his hand, aroused by its strength and roughness.

KYLE'S TORTELLINI

Serves 6

Dough:

3 1/3 cups all-purpose flour

1 teaspoon salt

4 eggs, room temperature

Filling:

8 ounces ricotta cheese

1 egg white

1/2 cup Parmesan cheese, grated

2 tablespoons fresh spinach, chopped

1/2 teaspoon dried basil

1/8 teaspoon freshly ground black pepper

1/8 teaspoon fresh nutmeg

1. In a medium bowl, stir the flour and salt together. Make a mound and create a well in the middle. Use a fork to beat the eggs and pour them into the well in the center of the flour. Incorporate the flour from the inner rim of the mound. Knead the dough and add flour a little at a time until the dough is no longer sticky. Once the dough is soft and smooth, wrap it in plastic wrap. Set aside for 20 minutes to rest.

2. In a mixing bowl, add the ricotta, egg white, cheese, and spices. Mix well. Set aside.

3. Dust your work surface with flour. Cut a ¼-piece of the dough, keep the unused portion of the dough well covered until ready to use. Flatten the dough with your hands into a small rectangle.

4. With your pasta machine on the widest setting, pass the dough through 2 times, keeping it flat, dusting with flour as needed. Reduce the setting by 1 number and pass the dough through again. Repeat until the dough is thin and smooth.

5. Lay the dough out on your floured work surface. Using a 3-4-inch round cookie

cutter, cut circles and set on a floured surface. Brush the edges of the rounds closest to you with the water. Add 1 teaspoon of the ricotta mixture to the center of each. Fold the circle over the ricotta filling to meet the other side. Press firmly to seal. Bring the corners around to the bottom to meet and stick them together using egg wash. Let the tortellini dry in a single layer on a parchment lined sheet pan dusted with flour for 30 minutes.

6. Bring a pot of water to a boil and add 1 tablespoon of salt. Drop the tortellini in the water and cook until they float to the top, about 5-7 minutes. Drain and toss with olive oil to prevent sticking.

Cheese Sauce

Serves 6

1/4 cup butter

1/4 cup all-purpose flour

2 cups milk

1 teaspoon Worcestershire sauce

1/2 teaspoon mustard powder

1 teaspoon onion powder

1/4 teaspoon cayenne pepper

2 cups shredded Cheddar cheese

1 cup shredded parmesan cheese

1. Melt butter in a large pot over medium-low heat. Add flour, whisking constantly; cook until golden and the mixture no longer smells of flour, about 5 minutes. Slowly pour the milk into the flour mixture, whisking continually until fully incorporated.
2. Stir in Worcestershire sauce, mustard powder, onion powder, and cayenne pepper. Season with salt and black pepper.
3. Reduce heat to low. Cook sauce, whisking frequently, until it begins to thicken, about 6 minutes.
4. Add the cheeses; stir continually until the cheese melts completely. Remove sauce from heat. Pour over drained pasta and serve.

4

APPLES

*C*asi pulled out two cokes and handed one to Kyle, assuming he would prefer it to Alix's array of healthy beverages. "Excellent." Kyle smiled as he observed the almost empty fridge. "What's the story on the apple?"

"I found it at a produce stand the other day." She contemplated the lonely fruit. "It was expensive." She smiled at the sticker which read, Washington. "Hey, it's from your homeland!"

"Most apples are."

She removed the sticker and washed it before slicing it directly on the granite counter, making him cringe. She arranged the pieces on a paper towel and sat, indicating a stool beside her. "I'm breaking up with Alix."

Kyle put his hand on her arm. "Are you ok? You don't seem happy about it," he said with concern.

She wiped a tear away. "I'm happy, but I'm anxious about my career. I'm turning thirty in a few months."

He reached over and touched her cheek, wiping away a new tear with his thumb. "It might be a good time to make some changes." He pulled her closer, loving the weight of her in his arms as if she belonged there.

ALIX'S APPLE CRUMBLE

Serves 12

Filling:

4 granny smith apples, peeled and diced

2 tablespoons lemon juice

1/2 cup brown sugar

2 tablespoons flour

1 teaspoon cinnamon

1/2 teaspoon cloves

1/2 teaspoon salt

1 teaspoon vanilla

Crumble:

3/4 cup butter-melted

1 cup firmly packed brown sugar

1 1/2 cups all-purpose flour

1/2 teaspoon baking soda

1/2 teaspoon salt

1 1/2 cups old fashioned rolled oats

1. Mix the apples with lemon juice, sugar, flour, spices, and vanilla. Set aside. In a bowl, mix brown sugar, flour, baking soda, salt, and oats. Stir in butter and mix until crumbly.

2. Press half the topping evenly over the bottom of a buttered 9 x 13-inch baking pan. Spread apple mixture on top and sprinkle remaining crumble over apples.

3. Bake in a 375-degree oven until the crisp is lightly browned, 20 to 25 minutes. Place pan on a rack to cool for about 10 minutes. While still warm, cut into 12 pieces. Let cool completely in pan.

CALVADOS CARAMEL SAUCE

Makes 2 cups

1 cup white sugar

1/2 cup water

3/4 cup heavy whipping cream

2 tablespoons Calvados (Apple brandy)

3 tablespoons unsalted butter

1/4 teaspoon sea salt

1. Pour sugar and water into a small saucepan; swirl gently to combine. Heat over medium-low heat until little bubbles form on the side. Do not stir.
2. Increase heat to high and boil until sugar turns amber, 5 to 8 minutes. Remove from heat and carefully whisk in heavy cream and Calvados. Add butter and salt, stirring to combine. Let cool slightly before serving.

5

LIFE'S A BEACH

*C*asi had a sudden sensation of flying, twisting madly in the air before she skidded to a stop while grazing over the uneven surface. *What just happened?* Thoughts raced through her mind, but everything became jumbled and fuzzy. A blur of a red sports car racing down the mountain road penetrated her fog. She tried to lift her head, but the pain tore up her spine and her legs were numb. She tasted the saltiness of blood and sensed the wetness of tears on her face, but she was shrouded in a cloud of uncertainty and confusion almost like a dream.

"Oh, my God, Casi!" she heard someone shriek. The warmth and coarseness of the gravel radiated through her and the vibration tingled along her spine as they ran toward her. Several voices sang out. "Don't move her, her back might be broken."

A bright flash sparkled before her eyes and she thought maybe an angel had come to escort her to heaven, then realized it was a camera. *Was someone taking pictures of her? Face down on the ground in a crumpled mess? Did she still have legs or had they been severed?* Hot, salty tears flowed down her nose and mixed with her blood in the gravel. She thought back to Kyle waving goodbye and all the possibilities life held minutes ago.

DYLAN'S ARTICHOKE PARMESAN DIP

Serves 6

Dip:

1 cup grated parmesan cheese

4-ounce mascarpone cheese

8-ounce artichokes hearts in water, drained and chopped

1/2 cup mayonnaise

2 ounces chopped, canned green chilies

1 tablespoon lemon juice

2 cloves garlic, minced

1/2 teaspoon tabasco

1 teaspoon fresh thyme

Crostini:

1/2 baguette, sliced into 24 pieces

3 tablespoons olive oil

½ teaspoon salt

½ teaspoon black pepper

1. In a medium bowl, mix together the parmesan, mascarpone, artichoke hearts, mayonnaise, green chilies, lemon juice, garlic, and tabasco.
2. Place the mixture in an oven safe glass pie pan or bowl and bake in a 350-degree oven for 20-25 minutes until it is bubbly and brown on top. Sprinkle with fresh thyme.
3. Place the baguette slices on a sheet pan. Drizzle with olive oil and sprinkle with salt and pepper.
4. Bake in a 350-degree oven for 10 minutes until golden. Serve with dip.

6

DAMAGE

*C*asi floated through the beeping and pinging of machinery, mingling with the aroma of antiseptic and roses tickling her nose. Her face felt puffy, and her body was hot and cold at the same time. She tried to speak, but she seemed disconnected from her body. Panic started to rise in her throat and her heartbeat quickened. The pulse of a monitor kept pace with her anxiety. She thought about pressing the call button but couldn't think of a valid reason. She tried to calm her mind and focus on her breathing. When a tall figure walked through the door, she burst into tears. "Daddy!"

"Oh, Sweetheart, I'm here." Jack embraced his daughter cautiously, observing the wires and tubes attached to her. "You can come back and stay with us and we'll take care of you." Casi hadn't considered her needs after being released. The pain kept her very present in the moment. They chatted for a while about her work, his restaurant, Ava, and their garden. After a while, the nurse came in to give her dinner and said visiting hours were over. Jack shocked her when he announced he would be staying with Sonya. He laughed and said, "We're on decent terms, Honey. She's one crazy lady, but we're civil if we can lead separate lives."

JACK'S STUFFED PORK LOIN

Serves 6

Roast:

3-pound pork loin roast

2 tablespoons olive oil

3 cloves garlic, minced

1 teaspoon salt

1 teaspoon smoked paprika

1 teaspoon black pepper

1/2 teaspoon cumin

Stuffing:

1/2-pound loaf artisan bread (pugliese), cut into 1-inch cubes

1/2 cup chicken stock

2 tablespoons butter, melted

1/2 cup dried cranberries

1 granny smith apple, peeled and diced

1/2 cup onion, diced

1 stalk celery, diced

1/2 teaspoon salt

1/2 teaspoon dried sage

1/2 teaspoon dried oregano

1. Preheat oven to 375-degrees. Line a sheet pan with tin foil and brush with vegetable oil.

2. In a medium bowl, combine the bread cubes, chicken stock, butter, cranberries, apple, onion, celery, and spices. Set aside.

3. Use a boning knife to pierce the pork roast in the center of each end. Sweep the knife from side to side to create a tunnel through to the center of the roast, leaving a 1-inch border around the sides.

4. Press the stuffing into the roast, starting at one end towards the middle and then from the other end. Make sure it is evenly stuffed. Combine the olive oil, garlic, and spices and rub evenly over roast. Place on the sheet pan and roast for about 1 hour. Temperature should read 145-degrees (make sure to check stuffing temperature). Remove from oven and tent with foil to rest. Slice the roast into 1-inch pieces and arrange on a platter to serve.

JACK DANIELS SAUCE

Makes 2 cups

1 cup chicken stock

½ cup Jack Daniels Whiskey

¼ cup brown sugar

4 tablespoons apple cider vinegar

2 tablespoons soy sauce

3 cloves garlic, minced

2 tablespoons butter

salt and pepper to taste

1. In a small saucepan, add chicken stock, whiskey, brown sugar, vinegar, soy sauce, and garlic. Bring to a boil and reduce to a simmer.

2. Continue to simmer until the sauce is reduced by half, about 10 minutes. Turn the heat off and swirl in the butter and stir until it is melted. Season with salt and pepper.

7

DISCOVERY

"I'm from Elmvale, Washington, originally. It's a tiny town, north of Bellingham. I moved to Blackberry Falls after college because of the beautiful lake, and its proximity to Seattle." Kyle gave Casi details about his family and how he graduated from the University of Washington, with a degree in business.

"I'm from Burnaby, Canada. Do you know where that is?"

"Huh? East of Vancouver. I wasn't aware you were Canadian. Maybe there's hope for you yet."

Casi considered her Facebook page. Modeling pictures, selfies, and 'aren't we awesome' poses with her friends at nightclubs. It said she lived in Hollywood, making her question when it would be appropriate to change her relationship status linked to Alix. She told Kyle more about her life before modeling, drifting off, her voice sounding muffled in her head. She liked the comfort of him being in the apartment as she fell asleep. As she started dreaming of being on the beach, he kissed her on the forehead and whispered, "Sweet dreams." She wanted to reach out for him, but sleep immobilized her.

RAY DAWSON'S NANAIMO BARS

Makes 12

Crust:

½ cup butter

¼ cup sugar

5 tablespoons cocoa

1 egg, beaten

1 ¼ cup graham wafer crumbs

½ cup blanched almonds, finely chopped

1 cup coconut

Custard:

3 tablespoons custard powder (or vanilla pudding powder)

3 tablespoons heavy cream

1 teaspoon vanilla

½ cup butter, room temperature

2 cups powdered sugar, sifted

Topping:

½ cup semisweet chocolate, chopped

2 tablespoons butter

1. In a double boiler, add the butter, sugar and cocoa. Stir until smooth. Remove from

heat and add the egg, whisking well. Add the graham crumbs, and coconut and stir until combined. Press mixture into the bottom of an 8 x 8 pan and set aside.

2. Combine the heavy cream, custard powder, and vanilla. Whisk in the butter, adding the powdered sugar slowly. Beat until smooth. Spread the custard layer on top of the crust layer, evenly.

3. In a double boiler, melt the chocolate and butter until glossy. Pour over the custard layer and quickly ensure it is well covered. Refrigerate for 1 hour or overnight.

4. Cut the bars into 12 even pieces.

8

PHOTOGRAPHS

"*D*arling, he's a workman! Lovely to have sex with, but don't get your hopes up for something more," Sonya said aghast. "I'm sure in his small town, he's a big deal. But this is LA and you're a beautiful girl who should be searching for a wealthy husband before your looks fade."

"Mother! I have no desire to be anyone's wife and I can take care of myself," Casi said defiantly.

"A romantic notion of the young and naïve, but you should be concerned about your long-term financial security. You know as well as I do, you will tire of his small-town charm."

Casi was not one of those inept women desperate to be a trophy wife, residing at the coffee shop, perpetually in yoga pants. *Did she see this going somewhere, or did his masculinity and blue eyes mesmerize her? Would she tire of him as her mother predicted and feel trapped by the normalcy of a relationship? What did Kyle want?* He made his attraction to her clear, but was he the marriage and children type, and would he be ultimately crushed when he found out she wasn't? She pondered whether she was being fair to him, flirting like a school girl. *What did she know about love?* In fact, she lived with Alix for more than four years because of his lack of commitment and emotional detachment.

SONYA'S BAILEY'S IRISH CREAM CAKE

Serves 12

Cake:

12 ounces unsalted butter, room temperature

8 ounce cream cheese, room temperature

1 teaspoon salt

2½ cups granulated sugar

2 tablespoons cornstarch

1 teaspoon vanilla extract

6 eggs, room temperature

3 cups sifted cake flour

1/2 cup Bailey's Irish Cream

Glaze:

1/2 cup butter

1/4 cup water

1 cup white sugar

1/4 cup Bailey's Irish Cream

1 cup pecans, chopped

1. Preheat oven to 325-degrees. Butter a Bundt pan and sprinkle with flour.
2. Cream butter and cream cheese in a bowl of a stand mixer using the paddle attachment. Add the salt and sugar and mix until smooth.
3. Add the cornstarch and vanilla, then slowly stir in the eggs. Alternate adding the Bailey's Irish Cream and flour, mixing well.
4. Pour the cake batter in the prepared pan and bake for about 40 minutes or until a toothpick inserted into the center of the cake comes out clean. Allow to cool in the pan for 10 minutes then remove and place on plate. Poke holes with a skewer to create tunnels for the glaze.
5. In a saucepan, combine butter, water and sugar. Bring to a boil for 5 minutes, stirring constantly. Remove from heat and stir in 1/4 cup Irish cream and pecans. Spoon the glaze over the warm cake. Slice the cake into 12.

9

FALLING

*C*asi opened her eyes to witness Kyle standing above her in the now darkened room. She stretched lazily and yawned, a smile still on her face from her earlier activities, and a vivid dream of him making love to her. "I picked up supper." He held up a bag of Chinese takeout in one hand and a six-pack in the other. "As a Canadian, I assumed you'd prefer beer with your Chinese. I noticed you're not taking your prescription, so your liver can handle a little alcohol."

"Aren't you observant," she mused as she lifted her foot toward him, letting her toes trail up the leg of his jeans.

"You have been doing your physical therapy," he said, not flinching as she continued her journey. "I also got you these." He produced a set of Egyptian cotton sheets. "Those satin things look uncomfortable as hell."

"After dinner activity?"

Kyle blushed deeply, realizing the unintended sexual reference the new bedding would suggest. "I don't think so, Miss broken pelvis...." he trailed off, removing her foot before it could reach his zipper.

ROBERT'S CREPES

Makes 12

2 eggs

1 cup milk

1 cup all-purpose flour

¼ teaspoon salt

2 tablespoons butter, melted

2 cup raspberries

1. In a blender combine eggs, milk, flour, salt and butter. Process until smooth. Cover and refrigerate 1 hour.
2. Heat a skillet over medium-high heat and brush with oil. Pour 1/4 cup of crepe batter into pan, tilting to completely coat the surface of the pan. Cook 2 to 5 minutes, turning once, until golden. Remove the cooked crepe to a plate. Repeat with remaining batter.
3. Fill the crepes with Chambord whipped cream and raspberries and drizzle with chocolate sauce.

CHOCOLATE SAUCE

Makes 3 cups

2 cups semisweet chocolate chips

1 cup sweetened condensed milk

1 teaspoon vanilla extract

1/8 teaspoon salt

1. In a large saucepan, combine the chocolate chips and sweetened condensed milk. Cook and stir over low heat until melted.
2. Remove from heat, and stir in vanilla and salt. Serve warm.

CHAMBORD WHIPPED CREAM

2 cups heavy cream

4 tablespoons powdered sugar

3 tablespoons Chambord

1. In a large bowl, whip cream, sugar, and Chambord until soft peaks form. Make sure not to over-beat.

10

BILLS AND PILLS

*C*asi responded to a tap on her shoulder and glanced into the ice-blue eyes of a Russian girl she recognized vaguely from past shows. "Take zis." She produced a large blue capsule. Casi shook her head and pushed the girl's hand away. "Da," the girl commanded, forcing it into Casi's palm with a firm nod.

Mary returned and touched Casi's forehead. "Honey, you're done, you can't continue. You gave it your best shot."

Casi thought of Kyle and how he had told her she wasn't ready for the catwalk, and the gaggle of girls sneering at her from the sidelines. She pictured the faces of the crowd gazing at her admiringly, loving her newfound curves and the sexiness she exuded. She put the pill in her mouth when Mary turned away and took a swig of water. She reasoned it would either work or kill her, but either way, if it made the pain stop, she would be thrilled.

Casi was warm and cold at the same time, but she couldn't feel her limbs. She stood, wondering if she had legs. She felt like a floating head and worried she may collapse, but oddly, her body knew what to do without her. She peered at the Russian girl, who gave her a pretty, knowing smile. Casi stepped out on the runway to the piqued interest of spectators anxiously perusing her new image.

NADIA'S PIEROGI

Serves 6

Filling:

2 russet potatoes, peeled and cubed (about 2 cups)

3 tablespoons butter

3 green onions, minced

½ teaspoon salt

½ teaspoon white pepper

Dough:

3 eggs

1 cup sour cream

3 cups all-purpose flour

1/4 teaspoon salt

1 tablespoon baking powder

Topping:

4 tablespoons butter

¼ cup shallots, minced

1. Bring the potatoes to a boil in a pot filled with enough water to cover. Cook until the potatoes can be easily pierced with a fork. Drain and remove to a bowl. Add butter while they are hot and press with a fork to melt the butter , keeping the potatoes chunky. Fold in green onions and season with salt and pepper. Let cool.

2. To make the dough, beat the eggs and sour cream until smooth. Mix the flour, salt, and baking powder together and add to the sour cream mixture. Knead the dough on a lightly floured surface until smooth, adding more flour if the dough is sticky. Roll the dough to 1/4-inch thickness. Cut 3-inch rounds using a biscuit cutter.

3. Place a small spoonful of the potato filling in the center of each round. Moisten the edges with water, fold over, and press together with a fork to seal.

4. Bring a large pot of lightly salted water to a boil. Add perogies and cook for 3 to 5 minutes or until pierogi float to the top. Remove with a slotted spoon.

5. Heat butter in a medium pan and place the cooked pierogi in to brown. Remove the browned dumplings to a plate. Add the shallots to the remaining butter and sauté for about 5 minutes until tender. Drizzle the butter and shallots over the plate of pierogi before serving.

11

CRASH AND BURN

The nightclub had a line around the block filled with hopeful partygoers. Casi exited the Uber and bypassed the line with a nod to the bouncer who opened the ropes for her. It was obvious she was a model, and her presence meant more money for the club, as eager men wanted to buy her drinks. Nadia sat with her crew, super-sexy in a black net top over a barely-there silver miniskirt. The bottle service girls moved aside and handed Casi a glass of champagne from one of several $200 bottles purchased for the group. For the next hour, she downed drinks and swayed with the music. Nadia pulled her toward the floor, and she obeyed, giving into the rhythm of the music as Nadia danced behind her, caressing her hips. She thought of Kyle and wondered if he was having a good time, wishing she hadn't been such a bitch. She let the music lead her into a sensual dance, making the men ogle them. The throng of the crowd and fog machine pumping an ethereal smoke into the room carried her to another dimension. The sharp bones of Nadia's frame pressed against her, and her heart beat rapidly. The air was too thick, and her throat constricted, choking her as blood surged through her veins like a levy let loose. Casi staggered forward. "I need air."

RILEY'S SWEET AND SOUR CHICKEN

Serves 6

3 boneless, skinless chicken breasts

1 cup mayonnaise

½ teaspoon salt

½ teaspoon ground black pepper

1 teaspoon granulated garlic

Coating:

1 teaspoon salt

1 cup cornstarch

1 cup all-purpose flour

Sauce:

1 cup sugar

½ cup ketchup

1 cup pineapple chunks with juice

¾ cup apple cider vinegar

1 1/2 tablespoons soy sauce

1 red bell pepper, cut into 1-inch pieces

2 cloves garlic, minced

1 tablespoon cornstarch mixed with 1 tablespoon water

Vegetable oil for frying

1. Preheat the oven to 375-degrees. Cut the chicken into bite-sized chunks. Mix with the mayonnaise, salt, pepper, and garlic. Set aside.

2. Combine the cornstarch, flour, and salt in a shallow bowl. Pour enough vegetable oil in a fry pan to coat the bottom and heat over medium-high heat. Dredge the chicken in the cornstarch mixture to coat well. Shake off excess.

3. Carefully transfer the coated chicken pieces to the hot oil. Brown evenly on all sides and remove to a sheet pan. Bake the chicken in the oven to ensure it is thoroughly cooked, about 10 minutes.

4. Combine the sugar, ketchup, pineapple, cider vinegar, soy sauce, bell pepper, and garlic in a saucepan. Bring to a boil and reduce to a simmer for 6 minutes. Add the cornstarch slurry and simmer until the sauce thickens, about 2 minutes. Pour the sauce over the chicken to serve.

12

CLUB GIRL

"*I* can't do this, Casi. I care about you so much. For God's sake, I'm in love with you." Kyle let the words sink in. "I can't sit here and watch you self-destruct. You're making one bad choice after another and pushing me farther away."

Tears sprung to her eyes, and she reached for him. He pulled his hand away. "Kyle! Don't leave me," Casi wailed.

"I'm heading back to Washington. My brother has a lot of work and I'm wasting my time here," he said with disgust as he strode toward the door. He glanced back and his shoulders slumped. "It sickens me to discover Jake was right about you."

A sob caught in Casi's throat as she screamed for him. Kyle brushed between the doctor and Mary as they stood outside the room. The doctor peered at Casi, giving her the once over, shaking his head as he walked away. Apparently, Mary convinced him not to report the incident, against his better judgment. Mary came in the room and touched her cheek. "Oh, Baby Girl, what are we going to do with you?" Casi let the tears flow and hugged her as if her life depended on it. Mary rubbed her back, gently rocking her. She understood Casi just lost Kyle, and it was only the beginning of a rough road she would need to travel down to face her demons.

TARA'S STREET CORN

Serves 6

1/4 cup butter, melted

2 tablespoons lime juice

1 teaspoon ancho chili pepper

1 teaspoon smoked paprika

1 teaspoon salt

2 ears corn on the cob, husked and cut in thirds

1/2 cup parmesan cheese

6 lime wedges

1. Preheat the oven to 375-degrees.

2. Combine the butter, lime juice, ancho chili powder, smoked paprika, and salt in a bowl; whisk until smooth.

3. Toss the corn in the butter mixture, coating evenly. Place the cobs in a baking dish and drizzle with any remaining butter. Sprinkle with parmesan cheese and cover the dish with foil.

4. Roast the corn in the preheated oven until tender and brown, about 30 minutes. Let cool for 10 minutes.

5. Unwrap the pan carefully and place corn cobs on a platter. Garnish with wedges of lime

13

BLACKBERRY FALLS

Kyle looked down to the beep of his phone. A notification from Facebook, another Casi Roberts selfie, posted for the world to admire. Long, muscular legs, topped by a thin strip of material, revealing toned abs and generous cleavage, barely contained in a midnight blue bra top. The hands of a man clasped her waist as they dirty danced. Casi's head was thrown back in ecstasy, haloed by a mane of streaked blonde waves. The caption read, "Rockin' my new do. Thanks, Dylan-love," with a hand-drawn heart.

He should have unfriended her weeks ago, tortured with every new post of her having fun, gorgeous and carefree. He wanted to not care about her anymore, to move on with a woman like Mary Ann, predictable and plain. Casi needed someone like Alix, moody and artistic. Kyle lied to himself that he would block Casi as soon as he got home, knowing full well he would go online and search for her latest modeling pictures to fantasize to. He noted Jake watching him with concern and turned the screen toward him. Jake's eyes widened at the photo. "Damn, could she be wearing less clothing? She is even sexier as a blonde."

MARY ANN'S HERBED FOCACCIA BREAD

Serves 8

2 cups all-purpose flour

1 teaspoon salt

1 teaspoon dried basil

1 teaspoon dried oregano

1 teaspoon dried thyme

2 teaspoons instant yeast

1 cups warm water, 110-degrees

Topping:

1 teaspoon butter

2 tablespoons olive oil

1 teaspoon fresh thyme leaves

1 teaspoon fresh oregano, minced

2 cloves garlic, minced

flaked sea salt

1. In a medium bowl, combine flour, salt, herbs, and yeast. Stir well. Add the warm water. Using a wooden spoon, mix until the flour is incorporated. Cover the bowl with a plastic wrap and let rest until doubled in bulk, about 1 hour.

2. Lightly butter a 9-inch cake pan. Pour one tablespoon of olive oil into the center and coat pan up the sides. Place the dough in the pan, turning to coat with oil. Press into a flat disc to reach the sides of the pan. Cover and let rise until doubled in bulk, about 1 hour.

3. Preheat oven to 375-degrees. Drizzle remaining olive oil over the dough. With oiled fingers, press straight down and create deep dimples.

4. Sprinkle top with garlic, herbs, and flaked sea salt.

5. Bake the Focaccia for 15-20 minutes until golden and springs back when touched. Let rest 5 minutes and then invert pan and set Focaccia on a rack to cool.

14

ROAD TRIP

*C*asi found the exit for Blackberry Falls relatively quickly, admiring the quaintness of the town with tree-lined streets. She tried to channel Alix's confidence in universal truths and let destiny take over. She rounded the bend and caught a glimpse of the lake, sparkling in the early evening sun. Kyle's back porch stood out, picture perfect, with bright Adirondack chairs and planter boxes featuring a colorful array of flowers. He looked severely sexy, sitting with his legs stretched out in front of him. She could see he was smoking a cigar and drinking what was probably scotch, with his dog Colt beside him.

Colt came trotting over as she approached, but Kyle's gaze remained on the lake, lost in thought. She petted the dog on the head, amused by the feel of his floppy ears, like strips of velvet. She stepped gingerly on the porch, unsure of what Kyle's reaction would be. She fluffed her hair and smoothed her dress. Colt nudged Kyle with his nose, breaking his concentration, and he glanced up in her direction, his face registering surprise. She smiled, trying to remember what she planned to say. She practiced a full apology for her behavior, explaining her state of mind and the pain she experienced. She forgot everything as he smiled back.

GAIL'S COLESLAW

Serves 6

1 cup green cabbage, shredded

1 cup red cabbage, shredded

1 red onion, sliced

2 carrots, peeled and julienned

1 red bell pepper, julienned

Dressing:

1/4 cup white sugar

1 tablespoon mustard powder

½ teaspoon kosher salt

¼ teaspoon pepper flakes

1/4 teaspoon ground black pepper

2 tablespoons white vinegar

2 tablespoons balsamic vinegar

2 tablespoons water

1 clove garlic

1 tablespoon soy sauce

1 cup vegetable oil

1. In a large bowl, mix together cabbages, onion, carrots, and pepper. Set aside.
2. Add the dressing ingredients to a blender. Blend until smooth and season with salt and pepper.
3. Pour a small amount of dressing over the vegetables and toss to coat. Add more as needed.

15

THE BROTHER

One shot turned into two, and Casi's earlier nervousness washed away, and she turned it up a notch with her dancing. She ordered another drink, flirting shamelessly with the bartender who was being very attentive. Jake scoffed and Casi caught his glare. "What's your problem with me?"

"You're gorgeous, a face and body beyond words." Jake smirked. "When I saw the pictures you posted on Facebook, I cautioned my brother to stay away from you. A good-time girl out for her next victim is what I said. Too bad I didn't write it in a text though, so when you were trolling through his phone, you could have seen it. Kyle is way too good for you and you're trying to con him because you got bored in LA, or maybe you've slept with all the guys there and you needed a new one to sponge off. I wonder, Casi, are you still living with that boyfriend or are you taking care of yourself now?" When she didn't answer, Jake continued, "Just what I thought, you can't even quit your last sugar daddy before you reel in another sucker. I hope you can give him a good enough time in the sack to make it worth his while." He laughed when he saw the tears start. "You shouldn't have come here. Your kind belongs in LA."

JAKE'S LOUISIANA-STYLE PULLED PORK

Serves 6

Brine:

4 cups water

4 cups apple cider

1 cup apple cider vinegar

1/2 cup salt

1/2 cup dark brown sugar

3 tablespoons dry rub

1 teaspoon red pepper flakes

Dry Rub:

1 tablespoon onion powder

1 tablespoon smoked paprika

1 tablespoon granulated garlic

1 tablespoon chili powder

2 teaspoons salt

1 tablespoon ground black pepper

1 teaspoon cayenne

2 teaspoons dry mustard

1 tablespoon ground cumin

1/2 Cup dark brown sugar

3-pound pork butt, cubed into 4-inch chunks

1. Mix the dry rub spices in a bowl and set aside.

2. Bring the brine ingredients to a boil to dissolve the 3 tablespoons dry rub. Let cool to room temperature. Pour the cooled brine over the pork and cover. Let brine overnight.

3. Line a roasting pan with tin foil, extending well over the sides. Transfer the pork from the brine to the pan and generously sprinkle with remaining dry rub, coating evenly. Pull the foil around the pork and seal well.

4. Place the pork in a 375-degree oven for 2 hours. Open the foil and continue roasting until the pork is easy to shred and the internal temperature is at least 160-degrees, about 30 minutes more.

5. When the pork is cool enough to touch, shred the meat while mixing in drippings to keep it moist.

CHIPOTLE BARBECUE SAUCE

Makes 4 cups

1 cup ketchup

1 cup tomato sauce

1/2 cup brown sugar

1/2 cups red wine vinegar

1/4 cup unsulfured molasses

2 tablespoons chipotle chilies in adobo sauce, minced

2 teaspoons hickory-flavored liquid smoke

1 tablespoons butter

1/2 teaspoon granulated garlic

1/2 teaspoon onion powder

1/4 teaspoon chili powder

1 teaspoon paprika

1/2 teaspoon celery seed

1/4 teaspoon ground cinnamon

1/2 teaspoon cayenne pepper

1 teaspoon salt

1 teaspoon coarsely ground black pepper

1. In a large saucepan over medium heat, mix the ingredients together and bring to a boil.
2. Reduce heat to low, and simmer for up to 20 minutes. For thicker sauce, simmer longer, and for thinner, less time is needed.

16

REVISITING THE PAST

Over the years, Casi's primary contact with her Canadian friends had been Facebook. She crafted a somewhat false image of success in LA because she had a deep fear of failing and being labeled as the girl who could never make it in the industry. Her biggest concern after the accident was to be the tragic friend who could have succeeded had she used better judgment.

Joey jumped up and hugged her when she entered the restaurant. Dawn was amused by Joey's flirting and poured her a beer. The years melted away as Casi chatted with her friends, picking at fries and chicken. She could hear the Canadian cadence in her voice return as she became more animated, and the beer flowed. She wanted to take a mental snapshot; so much a part of something, a member of a group. Not like the crews at the clubs, assembled of beautiful girls to lure men, but really belonging. Sharing common backgrounds and core values. They talked naturally, like they were teenagers again, laughing about their early years. Casi didn't share too much about her life, mostly mentioning she was 'seeing' someone. No, not an actor or an artist, just a regular guy. Kyle would fit right in, drinking and laughing with her friends. Her attraction to him was no surprise; he represented so much of what was precious in her youth.

JOEY'S BISCOTTI

Makes 24

1/4 cup light olive oil

3/4 cup white sugar

1 teaspoon vanilla extract

1 teaspoon almond extract

2 eggs

1 3/4 cups all-purpose flour

1/4 teaspoon salt

1 teaspoon baking powder

1/2 cup chocolate chips

1 cup hazelnuts, chopped

1. Preheat the oven to 325-degrees.
2. In a large bowl, mix oil and sugar until well blended. Mix in the vanilla and almond extracts, then beat in the eggs. Combine flour, salt, and baking powder; gradually stir into egg mixture. Mix in chocolate chips and hazelnuts.
3. Divide dough in half. Form two logs (12x2 inches). Dough may be sticky; wet hands with cool water to handle dough more easily.
4. Place logs on a sheet pan lined with parchment paper, about 4-inches apart.
5. Bake for 25 minutes in the preheated oven, or until logs are light brown. Remove from oven and set aside to cool for 10 minutes. Reduce oven heat to 300-degrees.
6. Cut each log into 3/4-inch-thick diagonal slices.
7. Lay biscotti cut-side down on the sheet pan. Bake approximately 8 to 10 minutes, or until dry to the touch.

17

THE CONCERT

asi awoke to see Kyle sitting at the dining table, coffee in hand, watching her sleep. Colt slunk from the couch and walked to his master, sitting at his feet, waiting to have his ears scratched. Casi emerged from the blanket, wearing only underwear and a tank top, having removed her jeans and bra during the night because they were suffocating her. She wrapped the quilt around herself and sat on the chair across from Kyle. He poured her a cup of coffee and added cream. Her head pounded, and she was aware she had mascara smeared under her eyes and a severe case of bed head. Kyle had showered and was handsome, but tired. "Casi, I have a lot on my plate," he spoke calmly. "Jake's marriage is crumbling, and it affects me and our business. Lumber prices are sky high because of the drought and there's a pine beetle outbreak to deal with." She hadn't considered the factors impacting Kyle's business; she assumed he went to work every day and made beautiful cabinets. He put his hand on hers as a peace offering. Hopeful the next words would be positive, she reeled when he said, "This is not a good time for us. I can't take on your baggage, on top of what I'm already dealing with." He quietly added, "You're not even emotionally mature enough to tell me you love me." His voice broke and her heart literally ached.

FRAN'S CARAMELIZED ONION ORZO

Serves 6

1-pound orzo

1 tablespoon salt

2 tablespoons butter

1 onion, diced

1/4 teaspoon salt

1/4 teaspoon sugar

1/2 red bell pepper. diced

2 tablespoons olive oil

1/2 cup pecan pieces, toasted

1 tablespoon parsley, minced

1. Bring 8 cups water to a boil in a large saucepan. Add 1 tablespoon salt. Add orzo and boil for about 5 minutes until pasta is tender. Drain and transfer to a medium bowl.
2. Heat the butter in a medium sauté pan. Add the onion and toss to coat. Sprinkle with salt and continue to cook over medium heat until the onion is lightly golden. Sprinkle with sugar and cook until medium brown. Add red bell pepper and sauté an additional 4 minutes.
3. Remove from heat and toss the onion mixture with the orzo.
4. Add the pecans and parsley and additional olive oil if needed. Season with salt and transfer to a medium serving platter.

18

TEARS AND TRIUMPH

The next few months were a flurry of activity. Casi enrolled in the classes Ava had suggested and balanced the courses between shoots and castings. She opted for the Business Management track, which she hoped would help her manage her career and provide future opportunities.

Casi's offer was accepted on a loft on Wilshire and she moved in her meager belongings. Inspired by Ava's beautifully decorated home, she talked Dylan into going to flea markets with her on the weekends after brunch. She bought a queen-sized bed and spent a fortune on 1500 thread count sheets. She had one chair, a find from the flea market, which almost killed them as they tried to carry it up the stairs, stopping every other step in a fit of laughter. A pretty pine desk in the corner was a treasure from the antique store on Vine. She set it up to do her schoolwork, putting it at an angle to the window, wanting to watch the world bustling around a few floors below while she sat perched in her sanctuary. She added an antique pine hutch to feature her tea cups, liking how it added charm to the room. Her bathroom exploded with a beach motif, including candles and shells. It smelled like coconuts and reminded her of being on vacation.

AVA'S PORK SCHNITZEL

Serves 6

2 pounds pork tenderloin, sliced into 6 pieces

1 cup all-purpose flour

1 teaspoon granulated garlic

½ teaspoon salt

½ teaspoon pepper

½ teaspoon paprika

3 eggs

1 tablespoon vegetable oil

3 cups breadcrumbs

1 cup parmesan cheese, grated

1/4 cup oil for frying

1. Lightly pound the pork into cutlets about ½-inch thick.

2. Combine the flour, garlic, salt, pepper, and paprika in a small bowl. In another bowl, mix the egg and oil. In a third bowl, combine the breadcrumbs and parmesan.

3. Dredge the cutlets in flour mixture, then dip in eggs, and press into breadcrumbs. Place on a sheet pan lined with parchment.

4. Heat oil in a heavy skillet over medium heat. Fry the breaded cutlets until golden brown, about 5 minutes on each side. Transfer to a wire rack over a pan and keep warm until ready to serve.

SPÄTZLE

Serves 6

3 cup all-purpose flour

½ teaspoon salt

½ teaspoon ground white pepper

1/4 teaspoon ground nutmeg

1/4 cup milk

2 eggs

1 tablespoon butter

1 tablespoon Italian parsley, minced

1. Mix flour, salt, white pepper, and nutmeg in a medium bowl.

2. Combine eggs and milk in a small bowl and add to flour mixture. Mix until smooth. Let rest 20 minutes.

3. Bring a pot of water to a boil and add 1 tablespoon of salt. Oil a spätzle maker or large colander and hold it over the boiling water. Transfer the dough and press through the holes into the water. Stir gently and let cook for about 5-8 minute until the dough is cooked through.

4. Drain the spätzle and toss with butter and parsley.

MUSHROOM CREAM SAUCE

Makes 3 cups

2 tablespoons butter

1 cup cremini mushrooms, sliced

½ teaspoon salt

2 tablespoons flour

1 cup milk

2 cups heavy cream

½ cup parmesan cheese, grated

1. Melt butter in a small sauté pan. Add mushrooms and sprinkle with salt. Sauté for 4 minutes, until mushrooms are tender.

2. Sprinkle flour over mushrooms and cook for a few more minutes, slowly stir in milk and bring to a boil, stirring constantly. Add cream and simmer until thickened.

3. Turn off heat and add cheese.

4. Season with salt and pepper. Serve with spätzle and schnitzel.

19

COVER GIRL

*C*asi noticed her magazine on the end-cap of the check stand and held back to see if Kyle responded to it. She pressed herself behind him out of sight and tossed a copy with his groceries, watching the confusion on his face when he discovered it. "Wow, a dirty magazine and a bottle of Jack. Someone's having a party for one!" She said in a husky tone.

Kyle turned in shock toward the voice. "Casi!" His eyes glistened with happiness and he embraced her tenderly. "What are you doing here?"

"I thought I'd swing by on my way to see my dad."

"Do you have time for a drink or something?"

"No sorry, it's only a quick hello." She hid her grin.

"Well, it was good to see you." Kyle's shoulders slumped.

Casi's heart ached for the pain in his demeanor. She threw her arms around him. "That was a joke. I came to see you because I heard about Colt from Lia."

Kyle breathed heavily against the crook of her neck. "You run circles around me. Do you want to come over?"

"That would be convenient since I came to see you." She waited for him to grasp the concept.

LIA'S CHOCOLATE CUPCAKES

Makes 12

1 1/3 cups all-purpose flour

1/4 teaspoon baking soda

2 teaspoons baking powder

3/4 cup unsweetened cocoa powder

1/8 teaspoon salt

3 tablespoons butter, softened

1 1/2 cups white sugar

2 eggs

3/4 teaspoon vanilla extract

1 cup milk

1. Preheat oven to 350-degrees. Line a muffin pan with paper liners.
2. Sift the flour, baking powder, baking soda, cocoa and salt together. Set aside.
3. In a large bowl, cream the butter and sugar until light and fluffy. Add the eggs one at a time, beating well with each addition, then stir in the vanilla. Add the flour mixture alternately with the milk; beat well. Fill the muffin cups 3/4 full.
4. Bake for 15 to 18 minutes in the preheated oven, or until a toothpick inserted into the cupcake comes out clean.
5. Decorate with mocha buttercream.

MOCHA BUTTERCREAM

Makes 3 cups

1⁄3 cup strong coffee

1/2 cup sugar

1 tablespoon cocoa powder

4 large egg yolks

6 ounces salted butter, softened

1. Pour the coffee, sugar, and cocoa in a medium saucepan and bring to a boil. Reduce by about half (the mixture should have a syrup consistency). Transfer to a spouted measuring cup and let cool about 5 minutes.
2. In the bowl of a stand mixer fitted with a whisk attachment, beat the egg yolks until pale and thick, about 10 minutes.
3. With the mixer running on medium, carefully drizzle the hot syrup in the yolks and whisk until room temperature, about 10 minutes.
4. Begin adding the butter a little at a time until it is fully incorporated. It might appear curdled, but it will come back together as it whips. Continue to whisk the buttercream until it is smooth.
5. Transfer the buttercream to a piping bag fitted with a large star tip.

20

TOAST OF THE TOWN

$\mathcal{K}$yle took Casi to the wood shop, and she admired the old stone building, converted from a dairy, beautifully restored and bestowed with hanging flower baskets. A young woman sat at the desk as they came in and handed Kyle messages with a slight blush. Kyle muttered, "Thanks, Amy," lost in the notes. Jake took the liberty of introducing Casi to the receptionist as Kyle's girl-friend. A brief look of defeat passed through the girl's eyes, as she took in the gorgeous woman standing before her.

Kyle led Casi to the workroom to show her around. He pointed to a yellow line on the floor and told her when the machinery was running, she could not cross it. She laughed and then realized he was serious. She slid on a workbench and turned up her iPod, distracting them as they measured a frame. Kyle came over and kissed her. "You've had the tour, now hit the road." She wrapped her legs around him and swung her wrists over his shoulders, giving him a sultry pout.

"Um, Mr. Jensen..." Amy hesitated at the edge of the work table. "You have a phone call."

"Thanks, Amy. I'll be right there." He unwound Casi's legs from his hips. "You need to leave or I'll never get work done."

AMY'S THREE PEPPER CORNBREAD

Serves 12

1 1/2 cups cornmeal

2 1/2 cups milk

2 cups all-purpose flour

1 tablespoon baking powder

1 teaspoon salt

2/3 cup white sugar

2 eggs

1/2 cup vegetable oil

1/2 cup yellow bell pepper, diced

1/2 cup red bell pepper, diced

1 jalapeno, minced

1. Preheat oven to 375-degrees. In a small bowl, combine cornmeal and milk; let stand for 5 minutes. Grease a 9x13-inch baking pan.
2. In a large bowl, whisk together flour, baking powder, salt, and sugar. Stir in the cornmeal mixture, eggs and oil until smooth. Add the peppers and stir to combine.
3. Pour batter into prepared pan.
4. Bake in preheated oven for 30 to 35 minutes, or until a knife inserted into the center of the cornbread comes out clean.

21

HEADACHES AND HEARTBREAK

"The summer I graduated high school, everyone hung out at the river, ready for our lives to change as we headed in different directions. Jake had been at college for two years. My best friend, Grady, had big plans to travel the world, claiming he couldn't get out of Elmvale fast enough. His family was poor and life had been tough, but he was determined to make it, and convinced me to go with him. We bought backpacks and created an itinerary to travel to Europe. He wrote that in my yearbook." Kyle ran a finger over the tattoo on his ribs, *Dare to Dream, Hope, Trust, Seek, and most of all, Love.*

"We had a blow-out party on the last day of summer. We were invincible, speeding around in our boats and having fun." He paused for a long moment and Casi feared where this might go, remembering him mentioning the scars from a boating accident. "I woke up in the hospital, my mother crying beside me, and my dad convinced I wouldn't make it. Jake was a wreck, and told me about the accident and how four kids died, and Grady was one of them."

GRADY'S CHEDDAR BISCUITS

Makes 12

2 cups all-purpose flour

1 tablespoon sugar

1 tablespoon baking powder

2 teaspoons garlic powder

1/2 teaspoon kosher salt

1/4 teaspoon cayenne pepper

1 cup buttermilk

1/2 cup unsalted butter, melted

1 1/2 cups shredded sharp cheddar cheese

Topping:

3 tablespoons unsalted butter, melted

1 tablespoon Italian parsley leaves, minced

1/2 teaspoon garlic powder

1. Preheat oven to 375- degrees. Line a baking sheet with parchment paper.
2. For the topping, whisk butter, parsley and garlic powder in a small bowl. Set aside.
3. In a large bowl, combine flour, sugar, baking powder, garlic powder, salt and cayenne pepper.
4. Whisk buttermilk with butter. Pour mixture over dry ingredients and stir until moist. Gently fold in cheese.
5. Scoop the dough onto the prepared baking sheet. Place into oven and bake for 10-12 minutes, or until golden brown. Brush the tops of the biscuits with the butter mixture.

22

TAKING FLIGHT

"I'm going to LA with Casi." Kyle stated.

Jake grasped the counter and exhaled. "For how long?"

"I'm not sure." Kyle squeezed his shoulder. "I need to be with her, even if it's for a week. I'm not ready to say goodbye."

"I understand." Jake nodded. "I can't handle it anymore, we have to sell the business." He looked toward the bedroom and whispered, "The panic attacks have become really bad. I'm sorry I'm letting you down, but I'm headed toward another breakdown."

"I'll help you get through this." Kyle smiled as Casi returned and wrapped his arms around her.

Jake smoothed his thumb over her jaw. "Is that bruise from yesterday? You said she wasn't hurt. They claimed they were paid to scare her." He paced the kitchen and breathed heavily. "I'm done with Gail. She can take it all and I'll live in a trailer. My kids don't need me at home anymore."

Casi grabbed his arm. "Why don't you come with us to LA? My mom's attorney has represented her through three divorces and she's always done alright. You could get an idea of what to expect and how to protect the business. My mom owes me a huge favor for meddling so the consultation would be free."

69

REID'S BROWN SUGAR BEANS

Serves 6

6 slices bacon, diced

1 red onion, diced

1 red bell pepper, diced

2 cloves garlic, minced

1 cup beef stock

1 cup ketchup

1 cup brown sugar

1/4 cup molasses

1 can black beans, drained

1 can white beans, drained

1 can pinto beans, drained

1. Preheat oven to 375-degrees. Grease a 9x13-inch baking dish with butter and set aside.
2. Heat a large skillet over medium-high heat and add the bacon. Sauté until crispy and remove to the side. Add the onion and bell pepper and cook until tender, about 5 minutes. Add the garlic and sauté another 3 minutes.
3. In a large bowl, stir stock, ketchup, brown sugar, and molasses together, then add beans and mixture from skillet.
4. Transfer the mixture to the prepared baking dish.
5. Bake in the preheated oven until bubbling and browned, about 30 minutes.

23

LAWYERS AND LOFTS

There was a knock on the door, and Jake answered it to find a handsome Argentinian, holding a leather jacket. He opened the door wider and turned down the radio, announcing Alejandro's arrival. Casi's cheeks burned as Alejandro relayed in his soft, lilting accent, "You forgot your jacket at my place Sunday morning when you left. I tried calling you, but it goes to voicemail." He explained he and Casi dated, giving too many details on how she came over after the club.

Kyle extended his hand and took her jacket. "Hi, I'm Kyle. As of Sunday afternoon, I'm Casi's boyfriend. Thanks for dropping this off." He closed the door as Alejandro walked away in confusion.

Casi rushed to the bathroom and splashed water on her face, trying to dispel the redness of her cheeks. She studied Kyle in the mirror. "I didn't lie about being in love with you, Kyle. You're the only man I want to be with."

"I know." He nuzzled her neck. "You have been for a while. You were too afraid to admit it. All that matters is what happened after you came to Blackberry Falls."

ALEJANDRO'S JALAPENO POPPERS

Makes 24

Filling:

8 ounces cream cheese, softened

8 ounces cheddar cheese, grated

¼ cup parmesan cheese, grated

12 jalapeño peppers, seeded and halved

Coating:

2 eggs, well beaten

1 cup all-purpose flour

¼ cup olive oil

1 cup dry breadcrumbs

¼ cup parmesan cheese

1. In a medium bowl, mix the cream cheese, cheddar, and parmesan. Spoon the mixture evenly into the jalapeno pepper halves.
2. Dip the stuffed jalapenos in the eggs and then coat well with flour. Place in a parchment lined sheet pan to dry for 10 minutes.
3. Dip the peppers into the oil and coat well. Mix the breadcrumbs with the ¼ cup parmesan cheese and press the peppers into the bread crumb mixture and place back on the sheet pan cut side up.
4. Bake the poppers in a preheated 400-degree oven for 10-15 minutes until golden and the peppers are tender.

24

NIGHTLIFE

The car dropped them in front of the nightclub where a long line wound around the corner. Kyle groaned, hating the whole scene. Casi exited the car with practiced grace, never revealing what she wore beneath her skimpy skirt. She laced her fingers through Kyle's and took the lead, past the line, and up to the front. Lia scrambled to keep pace, aware she would never get in on her own. The no-neck bouncer opened the rope and let them pass with a nod, closing it back after Jake. Casi sauntered up the steep stairwell with ease and crossed the dance floor to private seating. A U-shaped leather sofa defined the area. Models lounged, glued to their phones, the blue light casting an unnerving creepiness to their emaciated faces. A bar dominated the center of the lounge, serviced by scantily clad women in bustiers and hot pants. As Casi entered, space materialized and champagne was distributed. Kyle felt uncomfortable in the setting and he chugged the champagne.

"Easy there, Cowboy, we have a long night ahead of us." Casi nudged him.

"I might get lost on my way back from the bathroom and go hang out with stoners in the parking lot." Kyle grinned.

ANNA'S TERIYAKI CHICKEN WINGS

Serves 6

3 pounds chicken wings or drumettes

Marinade:

1 cup water

1 cup soy sauce

1 cup white sugar

1/2 cup pineapple juice

1/4 cup vegetable oil

¼ cup toasted sesame oil

1 tablespoon garlic, minced

1 tablespoon ginger, minced

Garnish:

¼ green onions, minced

2 tablespoons toasted sesame seeds

1. Whisk the marinade ingredients together in a large bowl until the sugar has dissolved. Add the chicken wings, coat with the marinade, cover the bowl with plastic wrap, and marinate in the refrigerator for at least 1 hour.
2. Preheat an oven to 350-degrees. Remove the chicken wings from the marinade and transfer to a sheet pan lined with parchment paper. Bake for 30 minutes until brown and crispy.
3. Pour the remaining marinade in a medium saucepan and bring to a boil for 5 minutes.
4. Place the cooked chicken wings on a platter and drizzle with marinade. Garnish with green onions and sesame seeds.

25

SAND AND SURF

*C*asi caught a cab and arrived at Coffee Bean three minutes early. The owners of the club were investors who liked to help small businesses get ahead. Alix met them at one of his installments, mentioning his friend Johan's swimwear and surfing supply company, Sand and Surf. Johan was from South Africa and wanted to build a business based out of LA. They were interested in Casi as the model to represent the brand, having been impressed with her magazine cover and layout. Johan especially liked the rawness of her images, the lack of retouching, and how her scars were visible. He insinuated he would like to see her scars up close and personal. She engaged, flirting with the investors and letting Johan put his hand on her knee. The deal Alix proposed would give her ten percent of the company, which could prove to be lucrative. After the meeting, she shook hands with the investors, turning her cheek as Johan leaned in for a kiss.

SAND AND SURF BOUILLABAISSE

Serves 6

4 tablespoons olive oil

1 leek, sliced

1 cup yellow onion, sliced

1 large Yukon gold potato, sliced

3 cloves garlic, minced

1 fennel bulb, sliced

1 teaspoon fresh thyme

1 teaspoon orange zest

½ teaspoon red pepper flakes

1 teaspoon sea salt

½ teaspoon saffron, crushed

6 cups vegetable stock

1 cup white wine

1 (15-ounce can) diced tomatoes, with juice

1-pound mussels, cleaned and debearded

1-pound cod or halibut, cut into 1-inch cubes

1-pound fresh shrimp, peeled and deveined

1. Heat the olive oil in a large saucepan, add leek, onion, potato, garlic, fennel, thyme, orange zest, pepper flakes, salt, and saffron. Sauté over medium heat for about 8 minutes until the vegetables are tender.
2. Pour in the vegetable stock, wine, and tomatoes with the juice, and bring to a boil for 5 minutes. Reduce to a simmer and add the seafood. Stir gently until the seafood is cooked through, about 6 minutes.
3. Adjust the seasoning and serve with a dollop of rouille on top.

ROUILLE

Makes 1 cup

1 red bell pepper, charred, seeded and peeled

½ teaspoon cayenne pepper

1 tablespoon fresh lemon juice

1 garlic clove, peeled

1/4 cup fresh breadcrumbs

1/4 cup fresh parsley leaves

1/2 teaspoon sea salt

1/3 cup extra-virgin olive oil

1. Place the bell pepper, cayenne, lemon juice, garlic, breadcrumbs, parsley, and salt in a blender. Puree until smooth. Slowly add the olive oil while processing to form a paste.
2. Serve with bread or add to the bouillabaisse to thicken and season the broth.

26

SHARKS

*J*ohan greeted Casi with a kiss before she could turn and say, "This is my boyfriend, Kyle, and he came to watch the shoot." He visibly sized up Kyle, shaking his hand cautiously. Johan remarked he might be a distraction for Casi and Alix insisted he would make her even sexier as she taunted him while she posed.

Kyle settled in the sand, trying to keep out of the way while she worked. The prep work was tedious, and he didn't understand why it took so long to get ready. She was perfect already. He watched them wet her hair, putting on a mountain of product to make it tousled with waves. Spray, crimp, and twist. Her body was oiled and bronzed, the makeup kept to a minimum. A sultry smudge of eyeliner and waterproof mascara, then layers of lip gloss, and bronzed cheeks to appear as if she stepped out of the surf. She removed her robe and stood with her back to him, wearing only tiny bikini bottoms. He watched Johan salivating and wanted to punch him. Oblivious to the attention, Casi patiently got tugged into a bright pink, shorty wetsuit. They left it unzipped, arranging her cleavage. *That's not practical. Why would anyone not zip up a wetsuit if they were surfing? It defeats the purpose,* Kyle thought.

JOHAN'S BOHEMIAN KOLACHES

Makes 12

1 package (.25-ounce) active dry yeast

½ cup sugar

1 cup whole milk, warm (110-degrees)

2 eggs yolks, room temperature

2 tablespoons butter, softened

3 cups all-purpose flour

1 teaspoon salt

1 egg white, beaten with 1 teaspoon water

1. In a small bowl, dissolve the yeast and sugar in the warm milk. Let stand for about 10 minutes, until foamy. Add the egg yolks and butter and stir well to combine.
2. Add the flour and salt while stirring to make a soft dough. Turn out on to a floured surface and knead until the dough is no longer sticky, adding additional flour as needed.
3. Place the dough in an oiled bowl and cover with plastic wrap. Let rise until doubled in bulk, about 1 hour. Punch the dough down to redistribute the yeast and allow to rise another hour until doubled again.
4. Roll the dough on a floured surface to ½-inch thickness. Cut circles with a 3-inch cutter and place the rounds on a sheet pan lined with parchment paper. Let rise until doubled, about 45 minutes.
5. Firmly press indentations in the center of each circle to create a deep recess. Fill the indent with 1 heaping tablespoon of strawberry jam. Brush the edges of the pastry with the egg white.
6. Bake at 350-degrees until the pastries are golden brown, about 10-15 minutes.

STRAWBERRY JAM

Makes 2 cups

1 pound fresh strawberries, hulled

2 cups white sugar

2 tablespoons lemon juice

2 teaspoons vanilla extract

1. Chop strawberries until you have 4 cups of mashed berries. In a heavy bottomed saucepan, mix together the strawberries, sugar, and lemon juice. Stir over low heat until the sugar is dissolved. Increase heat to high, and bring the mixture to a full rolling boil. Boil, stirring often, until the mixture reaches 220-degrees.
2. Remove from heat and add vanilla. Let cool.

27

PAPERWEIGHT

*J*ake packed while Gail stood at the end of the bed and watched him. "You don't mind if I take my clothes, do you?" he asked sarcastically.

Olivia stared at him with tears running down her face. "Why do you have to leave, Dad?"

"We talked to you about how this would work. You and Reid will live with Mom, but you can come and visit me anytime you feel like it."

"I don't want you to move out," Olivia cried.

"It will be hard in the beginning, but we'll all be happier if Mom and I aren't living together." Jake zipped his suitcase.

"Where will you live?" Reid asked.

"I'll stay with Kyle for a while, and then an apartment." He shivered at the idea of living alone.

Jake walked to his truck with his bags and Gail put her hand on his chest. "What happened to us?" she asked.

"We were only ever together for the kids."

"But we had good times, too."

"Not enough." He turned back and grasped her hand. "This was inevitable, neither of us should be shocked."

OLIVIA'S CHOCOLATE CHIP COOKIES

Makes 3 dozen

3-1/3 cups all-purpose flour

1-1/2 teaspoons baking powder

1 teaspoon baking soda

1 teaspoon salt

1-1/2 cups butter, softened

1-1/2 cups packed brown sugar

2/3 cup white sugar

2 eggs

2 teaspoons vanilla extract

2 ½ cups chocolate chips

1 cup peanut butter chips

1. Preheat the oven to 350-degrees.

2. Combine the flour, baking powder, baking soda, and salt; set aside.

3. In a medium bowl, cream the butter, brown sugar, and white sugar until smooth. Beat in the eggs and vanilla. Gradually stir in the dry ingredients, then stir in the chocolate and peanut butter chips.

4. Scoop the dough on a parchment lined sheet pan in rows of 3 x 4.

5. Bake for 8 to 10 minutes in preheated oven. Allow cookies to cool on baking sheet for 5 minutes before transferring to a wire rack to cool completely.

28

KITTENS AND CLOSETS

Something soft touched Casi's arm, and she spotted a tiny kitten with big blue eyes staring up at her from Kyle's hands. "How darling! Can I name her Jezebel?"

"That's a terrible name, but she's yours and you can call her what you want. I'll simply oversee her care to make sure you don't forget to feed or water her." He petted the kitten's head.

"I love her!" Casi kissed her fat belly. "I've never had a pet. I always wondered what it would be like." She launched into a convoluted story on her history of wanting a pet and her mother's insistence of not allowing it, even when she was living in LA and paying the bills. She digressed to a discussion on Sonya's incessant desire to quash her dreams and put her down.

"Can you focus for a moment? I've been down on my knee for five minutes." Kyle fidgeted on the hard floor.

"Did you trip? I thought you were tying your shoe." She tickled the ball of fluff and giggled when she purred.

"I have bare feet." He removed the kitten from her hands while he untied a pink ribbon from its neck and held up a diamond and emerald band. "Casi, I'm trying to ask you to marry me, and you're not making it easy."

JEZEBEL'S ROASTED CORN SALAD

Serves 6

3 cobs of corn, husked

2 cups black beans, cooked and rinsed

1/4 cup cilantro, minced

1/4 cup lime juice

1 small red onion, diced

1 jalapeño, diced

3 cloves garlic, minced

1 teaspoon sugar

1 teaspoon cumin

1 tablespoon olive oil

1 teaspoon chili powder

1 teaspoon salt

1. Lightly oil the corn and place on a preheated grill. Roast all sides of the corn until lightly charred. Remove to a plate to cool. Cut the corn from the cob.

2. Stir in the remaining ingredients and adjust seasoning. Let rest for at least 20 minutes to let the spices bloom.

29

APPLE BLOSSOM ROAD

*T*hey drove up the long driveway, and Casi had butterflies in her stomach. A tall, slender man, with gray hair working in the garden, waved when they pulled in. A pleasantly plump woman with an apron on stood on the porch, eager with anticipation. Kyle parked and got out of the truck, coming around to open the door for Casi. She stepped out slowly, regretting her outfit. She should have remembered she was coming to farm country, not spending the day in LA. It had been warm when they left and she dressed in tiny white shorts and a leopard bra top, with a loose fitting black tank. She wished Kyle suggested she dress more demurely. Kyle shook hands with his father and introduced her. Peter gave her a genuine smile, making her like him immediately. They walked up the stairs to the wraparound porch. Georgia stepped forward and gave her son a hug, then turned to Casi, taking her in her arms, and welcoming her. Kyle sat on the porch swing and directed Casi to sit beside him, putting his arm around her.

"I didn't expect you to be blonde," Georgia commented.

"I'm naturally blonde. I dyed it for modeling, and it was a lot longer," Casi said nervously as she hid her ring with her other hand, not wanting to spoil the surprise.

GEORGIA'S SWEDISH MEATBALLS

Serves 6

Meatballs:

1/2 yellow onion, diced

1 1/2 teaspoons salt

1/4 cup milk

2 large eggs

1/3 cup plain breadcrumbs

3/4 teaspoon freshly ground black pepper

1/4 teaspoon ground nutmeg

1/4 teaspoon ground allspice

1 pinch cayenne pepper, or to taste

1-pound ground beef

1-pound ground pork

Sauce:

3 tablespoons butter

3 tablespoons all-purpose flour

3 cups beef broth

1/2 cup heavy cream

1/2 teaspoon white sugar

1/4 teaspoon Worcestershire sauce

1. Mix onion, salt, milk, eggs, breadcrumbs, spices, and ground meat in a medium bowl until well combined. Cover with plastic wrap and refrigerate for 1 hour.
2. Melt 3 tablespoons butter in a large skillet over medium heat. Whisk in flour and cook until golden brown, 4 to 5 minutes. Slowly whisk beef broth into roux.
3. Add the cream, sugar, and Worcestershire sauce and simmer until slightly thickened, 6 to 7 minutes. Season with salt and pepper. Remove from heat and set aside.
4. Preheat oven to 375-degrees. Line a sheet pan with foil and lightly coat with cooking spray.
5. Form meat mixture into 2-inch meatballs with wet hands and place them on the prepared baking sheet.
6. Bake in the preheated oven until browned, about 20 minutes. An instant-read thermometer inserted into the center should read at least 155-degrees. Transfer meatballs to the sauce and cook over medium-low heat until warmed through, about 5 minutes.

HOMEMADE EGG NOODLES

Serves 6

2 1/2 cups all-purpose flour

1 teaspoon salt

2 eggs, beaten

1/2 cup milk

1 tablespoon butter, melted

1. In a large bowl, stir together the flour and salt. Add the beaten eggs, milk, and butter. Knead dough until smooth, about 5 minutes. Cover and let rest for 10 minutes.
2. On a floured surface, roll out to ¼-inch thickness or use a pasta roller. Cut into desired lengths and shapes.
3. Allow to air dry before cooking.
4. To cook fresh pasta, fill a large pot with water and add 1 teaspoon salt. Bring to a boil. Carefully add pasta and cook until it begins to float to the top, about 6 minutes. Drain but do not rinse. Toss with olive oil to prevent sticking.

30

HOMETOWN

Georgia gave Peter a glass of lemonade and sat beside him on a blanket spread out on the grass. "What do you think of our soon to be daughter-in-law?" he asked.

"She's perfect for Kyle." Georgia beamed.

"I haven't seen him this relaxed and happy since before the boating accident. She seems to bring out the playful side in him." Peter watched Kyle tickling Casi's nose with a blade of grass as they sprawled on the lawn.

"It's heartwarming to see the boy in him again."

"She sure is pretty," Peter observed. "I wonder how Jake will handle this. I'm certain he never thought Kyle would get married, and he's used to having his brother to himself."

Georgia smiled. "I predict Jake will have his jealous periods. Kyle chose a woman who will understand his close relationship with his brother, maybe without even knowing it."

PETER'S GRILLED POTATO SALAD

Serves 6

2 pounds small red potatoes, scrubbed

¼ cup olive oil

1 teaspoon salt

½ teaspoon ground black pepper

4 eggs

4 slices bacon

Vinaigrette:

½ cup shallots, minced

½ cup celery, minced

3 tablespoons stone ground mustard

2 tablespoons honey

3 cloves garlic, minced

1/2 teaspoon salt

1/2 teaspoon freshly ground black pepper

1/4 cup apple cider vinegar

1. Cut the potatoes in half and toss them in a bowl with olive oil, salt, and pepper. Place the potatoes cut side down on a preheated grill. Grill for 15 minutes on medium heat, and turn over to cook the other side until they can be pierced with a fork. When cool, dice leaving skin on.
2. Place eggs in a saucepan and cover with water and bring to a boil. Reduce to a simmer for 7 minutes. Remove eggs from water, cool, peel and dice.
3. Add bacon to a skillet over medium heat. Cook until crisp. Remove bacon from pan, crumble, and set aside. Add shallots, celery, and garlic, and sauté until tender, about 6 minutes. Add stone ground mustard, honey, and cider to the pan. Continue to whisk until the vinaigrette has thickened slightly.
4. Mix the potatoes, eggs, and bacon. Drizzle vinaigrette over potatoes, gently tossing to coat well.

31
DOUBT

The next morning as they prepared to leave the farmhouse, Kyle's phone rang. "Hi, Lauren." He cringed and sat on his bed and held the phone away while she called him every name in the book. When she broke down in tears, he put the phone back to his ear. "I'm sorry this hurt you."

"Sorry? How the hell did you think it wouldn't hurt me? Did you run out and find the first woman you could to prove how you weren't going to be forced into a marriage with me?"

"I never planned on getting married," he reiterated. "I met her, and then everything changed."

"After more than three years with me, not to mention the ten years of friendship before that, and what I put up with while you were off and on again with Lindsey... you met another woman a week later, and fell in love?"

He rubbed his temple. "Yup, pretty much."

"You're a bastard, Kyle. I hate you!"

"Well, that sounds a lot like the night we broke up." He shrugged as she hung up without saying goodbye.

LAUREN'S GNOCCHI

Serves 6

1 (8 ounce) container ricotta cheese

2 eggs

1/2 cup freshly grated Parmesan cheese

1 teaspoon salt

1 teaspoon pepper

1 teaspoon garlic powder

1 ½ cups all-purpose flour

1. Stir together the ricotta cheese, eggs, Parmesan cheese, salt, pepper, and garlic powder in a large bowl until evenly combined. Mix in 1 cup of flour. Add additional flour if needed to form a soft dough.
2. Divide the dough into 4 pieces and roll each portion into 1/2-inch-thick ropes on a floured surface. Cut each rope into 1-inch pieces, and place on a lightly floured baking sheet. Place in the refrigerator until ready to use.
3. Bring a large pot of lightly salted water to a boil over high heat. Roll each gnocchi over the back of a fork to leave a deep imprint. Boil the gnocchi until they float to the surface, 1 to 2 minutes, then drain.
4. Pour pesto cream sauce over gnocchi while still warm and gently toss to coat.

PESTO CREAM SAUCE

Makes 2 cups

3 cups packed fresh basil leaves

½ cup pine nuts

4 cloves garlic

2 tablespoons lemon juice

3/4 cup Parmesan cheese, grated

1/2 cup olive oil

1/2 cup heavy cream

1. Combine basil, pine nuts, garlic, lemon juice, Parmesan cheese, olive oil, and cream in the bowl of a food processor or blender. Blend to a smooth paste. Season with salt and pepper.
2. Heat in a small saucepan and serve over gnocchi.

32

FETISH

The beer flowed, and the group took turns telling embarrassing Casi stories. "Remember when?" became the theme of the evening, and Kyle enjoyed hearing the antics she pulled in high school, skipping class, and her infamous dance parties. He was pleased to learn the woman he loved was the same fun-loving person, instead of an awkward geeky girl with bullying issues.

Casi surveyed her friends. "We have chosen to do a destination wedding. Will you guys be hurt if we only have our families?"

"Ah, but we invited you to ours and it was killer!" Joey whispered in her ear making her blush. "Seriously, run away to tie the knot. That damn thing cost our parents a fortune and we should have used it to buy a house instead."

"Totally! It took us years to save for the dump we live in." Dawn nodded. "We were in our early twenties and still in party mode. A lovely celebration sounds ideal. We can do a girl's thing when you get back and see the pictures."

"Thanks for understanding." Casi smiled at Kyle. "I am excited to be married to the love of my life but I'm not jazzed about planning and all the hoopla."

DAWN'S SAUSAGE PHYLLO TRIANGLES

Makes 18

8 ounces uncooked Italian sausage

8 ounces cremini mushrooms, diced

6 ounces shiitake mushrooms, diced

3 cloves garlic, minced

½ teaspoon fresh thyme leaves

1 (16 ounce) package frozen phyllo pastry, thawed

¼ cup butter, melted

2 tablespoons parmesan cheese, grated

1. Cook the sausage in a skillet over medium heat until brown and crumbled. Remove excess fat, leaving about 2 tablespoons. Sauté cremini, shiitake mushrooms, and garlic to the sausage and cook until tender. Add thyme and season with salt and pepper. Remove from heat and set aside.
2. Preheat the oven to 375-degrees.
3. Unroll the phyllo dough, and cut into three equal strips, about 3x12-inches. Place a strip of the phyllo on a cutting board and cover the stack of remaining sheets with a damp paper towel to keep them from drying out.
4. Brush the phyllo strip with melted butter and put a tablespoon of filling in the center at the far-left end. Fold phyllo dough over the filling to make a triangle. Continue folding back and forth in a triangle shape, like folding a flag. Seal the end closed with butter. Place the finished triangles on a parchment lined sheet pan. Brush the triangles with butter and sprinkle with parmesan cheese.
5. Bake for 15-20 minutes until golden.

33

LADIES WHO LUNCH

A few weeks later, they had a fat puppy from a breeder in Oregon. Another German shorthair, with brown and white spots. Casi had been asked to leave the training to Kyle since it was important for the dog to understand his commands while hunting. Often Kyle would slip in bed at night to find her cuddling the puppy and growing kitten, trying to hide them under the covers. "You're spoiling them," he said affectionately, relocating them to their beds, figuring they would make their way up momentarily, but hoping he could make love to her uninterrupted.

Kyle tried several names, still missing his buddy, Colt. Casi laughed as the dog jumped and spun in circles. "Good boy, Dingo." She clapped and encouraged him.

"Please don't call him that. He'll think it's his name."

"Call him what?" Casi asked with a sly smile.

"Dingo." Kyle cringed as the puppy came running. "Damn it." He raised an eyebrow at Casi. "You did that on purpose, you little sneak."

"It's a darling name, isn't it Jezebel?" She cuddled the cat who purred her approval.

"Thank God we are not having children." Kyle shook his head and gave the dog a biscuit.

DINGO'S LEMON TART

Makes 1, 9-inch tart shell

Crust:

½ cup butter

½ cup sugar

1 egg yolk

1 tablespoon heavy cream

1 teaspoon vanilla

2 cups all-purpose flour

¼ teaspoon salt

1 teaspoon baking powder

1. Cream the butter and sugar in a bowl with a wooden spoon.
2. Slowly add the egg yolk, cream and vanilla.
3. Mix the dry ingredients together and add slowly to the butter mixture until just incorporated.
4. On a floured surface, roll dough to 1/2-inch thickness.
5. Use the tart pan as a template to cut the dough into a circle, leaving a 1-inch border for sides. Carefully transfer the dough to the tart pan and press to fit. Poke holes with a fork to vent.
6. Place the tart pan on a sheet pan. Line the tart shell with parchment paper and fill with pie weights, rice, or beans.
7. Place in a 375-degree oven until the tart shell is puffed and slightly golden, about 10 minutes. Carefully remove the hot filled parchment paper and place the tart shell back in the oven, about 5 minutes. Let cool.

LEMON CURD

Makes 3 cups

3/4 cup fresh lemon juice

3/4 cup sugar

3 eggs

1/2 cup unsalted butter, cubed

1 tablespoon cornstarch mixed with 1 tablespoon water

1 tablespoon grated lemon zest

1 cup blueberries

1 cup raspberries

1 cup strawberries, sliced

1 kiwi, peeled and sliced

1. In a 2-quart saucepan, combine lemon juice, sugar, eggs, and butter. Bring to a boil, whisking constantly.
2. Add the cornstarch slurry and boil for 1 minute, until the mixture thickens.
3. Strain the lemon curd through a fine strainer into a bowl. Stir in the lemon zest and let cool.
4. Spoon the curd into the baked tart shell and arrange fruit on top.
5. Cut into 8 pieces to serve.

34

SUMMER'S END

"Want to go for a drive and pick blueberries?" They got in the truck and Kyle took Casi's phone and put it in the glove box as she stared at him in horror. "You can text Dylan anytime, I want you to pay attention to where we are. You're anxious to get back, but please give Washington a chance."

"That's fair." She realized she hadn't been anywhere except the lake. They stopped and bought a box of vegetables from one of the roadside stands. "What does your family farm produce?" Casi asked.

"It's a hobby farm." He elaborated when he realized that didn't clarify anything. "It used to be an apple orchard. My dad kept the ten acres with the house. His brother has fifteen acres on the other side of the river, and his sister sold the remaining acreage because she prefers to travel most of the time."

"Then how did your dad make a living?"

"He's a plumber. He had a shop with his best friend, Earl. They retired a few years ago. We aren't wealthy people, Casi, but we live a good life and plan well for our futures. I've been upfront about all my finances," he said sincerely.

She smiled at him. "I respect the way you live your life. I need a partner, not a sugar daddy."

EARL'S BLUEBERRY PANCAKES

Serves 6

3/4 cup milk

2 tablespoons white vinegar

1 cup all-purpose flour

2 tablespoons white sugar

1 teaspoon baking powder

1/2 teaspoon baking soda

1/2 teaspoon salt

1 egg

2 tablespoons butter, melted

1 cup fresh blueberries

¼ cup vegetable oil for griddle

Pure maple syrup

butter

1. Combine milk with vinegar in a medium bowl and set aside for 5 minutes.
2. Combine flour, sugar, baking powder, baking soda, and salt in a large mixing bowl. Whisk egg and butter into milk. Pour the flour mixture into the wet ingredients and whisk until lumps are gone. Stir in blueberries.
3. Heat a large griddle to medium heat, and brush with vegetable oil. Pour 1/4 cup portions of batter onto the griddle and cook until bubbles appear on the surface. Flip with a spatula and cook until browned on the other side. Serve with butter and pure maple syrup.

35

DOMESTIC GODDESS

"Jake, were you happy when you were first married?" Casi set the bread on the table.

He shrugged. "I wasn't thrilled to have a family and responsibilities straight out of college. After Reid, I got used to the routine. I went to work and Gail took care of the kids. I came home to a clean house with dinner on the table and the laundry done. I enjoyed the predictability."

"Gail said it was the best time of her life." Casi beamed.

"It's nice she didn't hate me the entire time."

"Her bitterness stemmed from feeling lost as the kids got older and she could see everyone else moving on with their lives." She noted the relief on Jake's face.

"Did Gail say she didn't hate me either?" Kyle asked.

"She feels you are too disciplined." Cast smiled. "Gail needs you to help her manage the money. She's afraid to ask you, but she's worried she's making too many mistakes and is unsure how to invest properly. She doesn't trust anyone but you to advise her. She says you're incredibly good with numbers and make sound decisions."

Kyle shook his head. "Tell her to come see me at the shop. I'll set up a plan for her, and Brian can do her accounting."

BRIAN'S CEDAR PLANKED SALMON

Makes 6

3 (12-inch) untreated cedar planks

1/2 cup vegetable oil

2 tablespoons rice vinegar

1 tablespoon sesame oil

1/3 cup soy sauce

1/4 cup chopped green onions

1 tablespoon grated fresh ginger root

4 cloves garlic, minced

6, 4-ounce salmon fillets, skin removed

1. Soak the cedar planks for at least 1 hour in warm water.
2. In a shallow dish, stir together the vegetable oil, rice vinegar, sesame oil, soy sauce, green onions, ginger, and garlic. Place the salmon fillets in the marinade and turn to coat. Cover and marinate for at least 15 minutes, or up to one hour.
3. Preheat an outdoor grill for medium heat. Place the planks on the grate. The boards are ready when they start to smoke and crackle just a little.
4. Place the salmon fillets onto the planks and reserve the marinade. Close the lid, and grill for about 20 minutes. Fish is done when you can easily flake it with a fork.
5. Place the reserved marinade in a small saucepan and bring to a boil. Reduce until thickened, about 5 minutes. Drizzle the marinade over the salmon to serve.

36

ISLAND ESCAPE

*J*ack redirected Sonya to the bar. "Let me get you a drink. Where's Burt? Headed for your fifth divorce?"

She downed a vodka tonic. "Why am I the bad guy for wanting what's best for my child? The daughter I practically raised by myself. You show up for the highlights and upstage me."

He sighed, tired of the argument. "Can we please make this week about Casi and Kyle? They're amazing together, even if you can't see it. He makes her happy, and she loves him."

"What's she going to do in Washington? Serve coffee like the dull girl Jake brought?"

"She'll need to transition in her career. She'll find her own way. Stop pushing her and making her feel bad."

"Her beauty will fade and he will leave."

"Kyle loves her. He sees more than just a beautiful woman."

"Banking on love never works." She glared at him. "I hope she's smart enough not to get pregnant or she'll find out how hard it is when he loves the child more than her."

Jack exhaled. "Casi wasn't our only problem."

LIBBY'S BITE-SIZED MEAT PIES

Makes 24

Pastry:

2 1/2 cups all-purpose flour

1 tablespoon sugar

1/2 teaspoon salt

2/3 cup shortening

1 cup water

Filling:

1/2-pound ground beef

1/2-pound ground turkey

1/2 cup shredded Cheddar cheese

1 egg

1/2 cup milk

1 teaspoon salt

1/4 teaspoon ground black pepper

1 tablespoon soy sauce

2 tablespoons breadcrumbs

1 egg mixed with 1 tablespoon water

1. Place flour, sugar and salt in the bowl of a food processor. Drop in shortening and pulse until it resembles cornmeal. Add water through the feed tube while pulsing. Stop when dough forms.

2. Press the dough into a log and cut in half. Cut the log into 24 pieces. Press each piece into a mini muffin tin, extending up the sides.

3. Roll the other half of the dough about ¼-inch thick. Cut 24 2-inch circles and reserve.

4. Mix the beef, turkey, cheese, egg, milk, salt, pepper, soy sauce, and breadcrumbs together until well combined.

5. Spoon the filling into the prepared cups and top with a pastry lid. Egg wash the tops and bake at 375-degrees until golden brown about 15-20 minutes.

PERSIMMON CHUTNEY

Makes 2 cups

1/2 cup apple cider vinegar

1/2 cup onion, diced

1/2 cup raisins

1/2 cup white sugar

1/4 cup lemon juice

1 tablespoon canned green chili peppers, seeded and minced

2 teaspoons fresh ginger root, minced

1 teaspoon lemon zest

1 teaspoon ground coriander seed

1/8 teaspoon ground cloves

2 Fuyu persimmons, peeled and chopped

1. In a large saucepan combine the apple cider vinegar, onion, raisins, sugar, lemon juice, chili, ginger, lemon zest, coriander and cloves. Bring to a boil over medium heat, stirring occasionally. Reduce heat to medium-low and simmer until mixture thickens, about 10 minutes. Add the persimmons and cook until tender about 5 to 10 minutes. Season with salt and pepper.
2. Remove from the heat and let cool. May be made a day or two ahead.

37

NUPTIALS

Kyle watched Casi walk through the grove and her beauty took his breath away. He knew she would not wear a traditional gown, only slightly concerned what she might come up with. He wanted her to have the wedding as she chose, letting her figure out what she needed to be comfortable with the union. She was a vision in cream lace over lavender silk with a beaded halter-style top. As always, she dressed perfectly for her body type, elegant with a hint of what would be revealed to him later. When she grasped his hand, a shock vibrated throughout his body, and his heart pounded in his chest. *This is the woman I waited for all my life without even knowing it.*

The ceremony was simple, about love and honor. Kyle whispered, "With you by my side, I will dare to dream, hope, trust, seek, and most of all, love." They exchanged rings and the minister placed leis around their necks and pronounced them man and wife. They strolled to the beach for a Hawaiian feast of grilled ahi, Huli-Huli chicken, Kalua pig, plantains, and rice, overflowing from beautifully garnished platters. Mai Tais were the preferred drink for most of the guests. The conversation, riddled with laughter, continued well after the meal finished.

HAWAIIAN ROLLS

Makes 15

1 cup warm pineapple juice

1/4 cup white sugar

1 tablespoon active dry yeast

1 large egg

3 1/4 cups bread flour

2 tablespoons butter, softened

1 teaspoon salt

2 tablespoons butter, melted

1. Butter a 9x13-inch baking dish.
2. Mix the pineapple juice, sugar, and yeast in a medium bowl. Let stand for 5 minutes until foamy. Add the egg and 1 cup of flour and stir until combined and smooth. Add the softened butter and salt then continue to add the flour and knead until the dough is soft and pliable.
3. Place the dough in an oiled bowl and cover. Set in a warm place until doubled in bulk, about 1 hour.
4. Divide dough into 15 equal pieces and form into rolls. Place rolls in prepared baking dish, brush with melted butter, and cover dish loosely with plastic wrap; let rise until doubled in volume, about 30 minutes.
5. Preheat oven to 375-degrees.
6. Bake rolls in the preheated oven until the tops are golden brown, 10 to 15 minutes.

HULI HULI CHICKEN

Serves 6

6 boneless and skinless chicken thighs

1/4 cup brown sugar

2 tablespoons ketchup

1/4 cup soy sauce

2 tablespoons dark rum

2 tablespoons pineapple juice

1 tablespoon ginger, minced

1 tablespoon garlic, minced

6 pineapple rings

1. In a medium bowl, whisk together the brown sugar, ketchup, soy sauce, rum, pineapple juice, ginger, and garlic.
2. Place the chicken thighs into the mixture and marinate at least 1 to 24 hours or up to two days.
3. Remove the chicken from the marinade. Reserve the marinade and put the pineapple rings in to marinate for 30 minutes.
4. Place the chicken on a pre-heated medium grill and cook about 8 minutes per side. The chicken will be golden brown and should read 165-degrees on an instant read thermometer. Remove to a platter.
5. Place the pineapple rings on the medium grill (reserve marinade). Grill each side until the pineapple is caramelized and has grill marks, about 5 minutes per side.
6. Pour the reserved marinade into a small sauce pan and reduce the mixture on medium heat until it thickens slightly, about 6 minutes. Spoon over the chicken on the platter.
7. Arrange the pineapple on top of the chicken thighs to serve.

GRILLED COCONUT LIME SHRIMP

Serves 6

1 pound uncooked medium shrimp, peeled and deveined

2 tablespoons coconut oil, warm

1/2 teaspoon salt

1 jalapeño, minced

1 teaspoon lime zest

1/4 cup lime juice

1/4 cup coconut milk

1/4 cup coconut rum

1/4 cup cilantro, minced

4 cloves garlic, minced

1/3 cup shredded coconut, shredded for garnish

8 bamboo skewers, soaked for 1 hour

Dipping Sauce:

1/4 cup sour cream

2 tablespoons coconut milk

1 tablespoon coconut rum

1 teaspoon lime zest

1 tablespoon lime juice

1 tablespoon ginger, minced

1 tablespoon cilantro, minced

sugar and salt to taste

1. In a medium bowl, toss the shrimp with the coconut oil and salt. Add the jalapeño, lime zest, lime juice, coconut milk, coconut rum, cilantro, and garlic. Let marinate 1 hour.
2. Thread 4 shrimp per skewer, securing both ends of the shrimp
3. Place the shrimp skewers on a preheated medium grill for about 4 minutes, turn and grill the other side. Place on a platter and garnish with the toasted coconut.
4. In a small bowl, mix together the sour cream, coconut milk, coconut rum, lime zest, lime juice, ginger, and cilantro. Season with sugar and salt. Serve with the coconut shrimp.

ULTIMATE MAI TAI

Serves 6

6 ounces dark rum

6 ounces coconut rum

6 ounces triple sec

4 ounces grenadine

1 cup pineapple juice

1 cup orange juice

1/2 cup lime juice

6 cups ice

6 orange slices

6 maraschino cherries

1. In a tall pitcher, combine the rums, triple sec, grenadine, and juices.
2. Fill 6 glasses with ice and garnish with orange slice and cherry.
3. Divide the Mai Tai cocktail between the glasses, and enjoy!

HOPE- BOOK TWO IN THE CATWALK SERIES

Happily ever after comes at a steep price as past relationships and betrayal threaten to destroy a marriage.

Newlywed Casi Roberts struggles to find balance between her career as a model, a failing business deal, and living between the quaint town of Blackberry Falls and the chaos in Los Angeles. Kyle Jensen questions his choice to follow his heart when everything he values is threatened and his new wife becomes a stranger.

Devastation, jealousy, and lies force Casi and Kyle to focus on what they cherish and believe in each other. They soon learn true bonds cannot be broken while loyalty runs deep. Through faith and sacrifice, Casi learns who she can trust and who she should fear. She navigates a new path, discovering the truest meaning of love and what is worth fighting for.

Family and friends suffer disturbing circumstances and devastating events, forcing them to make difficult choices. When secrets from the past begin to surface, lies unravel and relationships are shattered. Hope prevails when they learn to face their fears and open their hearts to the power of love.

The second novel in the Catwalk Series continues an epic journey of love, intrigue, and triumph, revealing deeper stories within the captivating saga.

Hope is available on Amazon.com

TRUST- BOOK THREE IN THE CATWALK SERIES

Death, deception, and demons from the past plague the idyllic union of Casi and Kyle.

Casi continues to polish her professional image and hone her business skills while focusing on the opportunities ahead. Determined to prove her worth beyond sizzling in a swimsuit, she leaves the superficial chaos of modeling behind. Unfortunately, money can't buy happiness for her mother, Sonya, who refuses to abandon her tumultuous lifestyle and settle into the picture-perfect world Casi created.

Kyle reveals dark secrets from his youth he hoped would stay buried. Seeking forgiveness, he trusts his unfailing love for Casi to overcome the painful memories. He adjusts to the whirlwind pace of their new routine, pushing aside jealousy and insecurities to become the ideal husband, brother, and son. Jake continues to battle challenges and troubled relationships, but still fiercely protects his bond with his brother and supports Casi emotionally.

When Casi is blindsided by a tragedy, she is left reeling from the grief it causes as deception is unveiled. She realizes the secrets her family protected may only be the beginning of revelations from her childhood. She questions the validity of her relationships and must learn to trust again. She embarks on a journey of self-discovery, needing to move beyond the anguish of delusion that torments her.

Standing on the precipice of a brilliant future and the illusion of the past, can Casi step forward or will the haunting lies swallow her back into a realm that is familiar?

Trust is available on Amazon.com

SEEK- BOOK FOUR IN THE CATWALK SERIES

Small towns hide big secrets when mysteries unravel from beyond the grave.

Casi returns her mother's ashes to her hometown in northern Canada to finally put her to rest. What she discovers is an unnerving and deadly coverup from her childhood. She searches for solace with Kyle by her side and is protected by old friends, igniting romantic interest and reuniting relationships.

Kyle wrestles with guilt from his past, revealing the truth behind his nightmares. Casi plans a trip through Europe to help him find closure and honor commitments.

When a dark secret erupts, Casi becomes a target of conspiracy and threats. She reacts impulsively, setting severe consequences in motion. Mary and Ava step in, forced to break pacts and divulge truths kept hidden for decades.

From Northern Canada through Europe, revelations threaten families and unearth mysteries which were better left buried.

Will the knowledge from a hidden journal destroy the lives of Casi and Kyle or can they choose their own destiny?

Seek is available on Amazon.com

LOVE- BOOK FIVE IN THE CATWALK SERIES

Love Triumphs Despite Tragedy and Jealousy

Dreams are shattered. Bonds are broken. Deception creates chaos and doubt. Will relationships withstand the crush of betrayal when the truth is discovered?

A summer wedding promises love and opportunity while an autumn union brings misery and distrust. When lives intertwine, and an affair is uncovered, prompted by a malicious motive, Kyle and Casi attempt to rise above the drama, desperate to preserve their unique bond.

Casi falls victim to a trauma that crushes her confidence as she is forced to keep secrets and defend the people she loves. As lies unravel, she is pressured to reveal the truth. Overwhelmed by the circumstances and convinced they are each responsible for the treacherous outcome, one brother goes off the rails while the other is caught between loyalty and love.

Will the belief in always and forever be enough to protect Casi's and Kyle's marriage, or will harsh circumstances finally overcome their faith?

The final book in the Catwalk Series finishes with shocking revelations and a triumphant conclusion

Love is available on Amazon.com

ABOUT THE AUTHOR

Canadian-born author, Suzy Quenneville-Orpin, has always had a vivid imagination and a keen desire to write. Suzy views the world through her own narrative, weaving in the fascinating challenges, triumphs, and lifestyles of the people she meets. An unapologetic daydreamer, Suzy's early experiences in Toronto and Woodland Beach, Ontario provided the perfect upbringing to fuel her creativity and discover the wonder of the roads less traveled. A move to the west coast brought new opportunities and a love for the Pacific Northwest.

Follow Suzy to discover more about the Catwalk Series.

www.facebook.com/sqorpin
   www.twitter.com/authorsqorpin
   www.instagram.com/sqorpin
   Website: sqorpin.com
   Email: sqorpin@yahoo.com
   Amazon: Amazon.com/author/sqorpin

Made in the USA
Columbia, SC
12 October 2020